Contemp

Imagery, Sound & Form in Lyricism

Candace Meredith

Creative Talents Unleashed

GENERAL INFORMATION

Contemplation

Imagery, Sound & Form in Lyricism

By

Candace Meredith

1st Edition: 2017

Creative Talents Unleashed

www.ctupublishinggroup.com

Publisher Information
1st Edition: Creative Talents Unleashed
info@ctupublishinggroup.com

ISBN-13: 978-1-945791-35-2(Creative Talents Unleashed)
ISBN-10: 1-945791-35-7

Credits

Book Cover

Raja Williams

Book Description

L.J. Diaz

Editor

Meredith Donaho

Dedication

Dedicated to my beautiful daughter *Lilian Victoria*

and my son *Paton Xavier*

Preface

As I sit alone in the room I'm in whether it be the sun porch, my own bedroom or the balcony of the hotel, I sit and write while extracting from within something that feels more profound than the simple function of thinking. Poetry stems from a contemplative moment that resonates deeply within and as I focus on an image, object or idea I turn it over in my thoughts to bring alive that "thing" on the page; in short, I write as I feel in the moment and rarely do I ever want to let it go – so I write it down and I keep that thought with me for as long as I need to so I can sense and feel beyond an ordinary thought.

Table of Contents

Table of Contents

Table of Contents

METAPHYSICS

Table of Contents

Table of Contents

MOMENTS

Saying it Simply

When she says it simply
they believe she is the
most beautiful. She believes
in her long history
of inadequacy – when she
carried home his next evening
meal, and let it fall, she
smeared the gravy back onto
the plate, and brushed her fingers
over the pebbles until each one
fell back into the dirt. She hoped
he would return home to nothing
less than a cool plate
of something to eat. She believes
that good efforts are wasted –
when she tried for hours upon hours
to wash the stain from great-
grandmother's quilt, but
the threading came loose and tore apart
from the seams, knowing grandmother's
fingers were like nails to touch:
iron bone she used to stitch
with hands that barely kept it together.
She believes in a long narrative
there should be something useful
to say, but the weather inside her
melted or removed all the fire. Wild,
it is, how she thought there might be
something miraculous someday. She thought
then, as she believes now, there might be
a tomorrow when all the good intentions
would come together, to form a collection
bowl of beliefs in others, and how true too

because she did not convince them.
Not forced but beautiful, and smart –
street smart, and educated. No more
anticipation, but pulled out of her pocket:
all those good things, like being the most
beautiful, because she says it simply.

Invertebrates

Nylon sheathe,
or a golden crinkle, a hue
of metallic, reflective,
turquoise – brittle
as the dust off bone.

An elk died there.
The beetle, sheltered in
Its carcass, an inch deep
between the coolness of mud
and the hot, dry, shell

of the beetles. It's home.
It's May – the heat still
permeates the dry, naked
bone. The beetles don't
know the difference.

The do fly, the beetles.
But clumsily, and haphazard
as the elk had been when
he, perhaps she, waded across
the water, clumsily and broke
its leg. A lone beetle,
and then the rest came.

Upon Winning

He is a gymnast –
the even bars, rings,
pommel; his body
is like gel in the
fabric of his life –
shaped and molded,
sharp as a crow's
beak and poignant
like glass before the
sound begins to break
free of what was silence
when he stepped onto
the mat – and then
landed there as perfect
as two pair of dice
or the lottery of
cheering – it is
the same, or similar,
when the ego
is detached and prefect,
like perfectly winning
when it was time.
And the final score
wouldn't matter much.

Arts Poetica

A picture.
A photograph
of wrought iron
symmetry;
a vertical landscape,
of a high-rise home.

A painting.
A still life,
an artist
among the roses.

A sculpture
of a nude
man cloaked
in a tapestry –
a hint
at discretion.

A stencil
of eyes peering
through the forest
and an Eagle –
praying.

1957

The flag is half mass.
The dog lays beneath
a skinny tree in a wide-
open yard. His thirst
is not satisfied; he
drinks from the fountain.
There is an expanse of
Milkweed; the voluptuous
purple bulbs are attractive;
a butter-colored butterfly
takes notice, bats its
wings and scuttles on by.
The orchard is dry; rotted
apples litter the yard.
The earthworms beneath
the dirt are happy; it's cool
there and its merely
dawn. *Going to be over
100 today* Condry stifles
a complaint. *Don't forget
to stop and pick the raspberries*
Ruby hollers back, *in a week
they'll be all dried up* she
says. *The fish are bite'n*
Condry says, *aint
got time for pick'n
raspberries* he snorts,
*gonna have fish for a week –
won't have the need for
no raspberries* he says,
kicks up the bucket and
walks toward the horizon,
fishing gear in tow.

The dog shuffles through the door –
the heat closing behind him.

Caught at a Sobriety Check Point

We, teenagers,
counted their faces
like they were shadows
stained on air.

And we watched
as one scribed the lessons:
like smothering ash.

And heard, on
occasion, the scratching
of his pencil on tablet –
as if his notepad-paper
flicked its own pages

and when his words
fell from the margins
our humiliation became
a moment, caught
with permanent pencil –

unable to erase time.

My friend had said:
Keep driving, just drive

but he called our mothers,
who had to leave the bar
with our fathers who were
too drunk to drive.

At Midnight

The tree-lined
streets are hidden
in the dark. Moon
Café is closed. A
solitary street lamp
flickers across this
quintessential little
town of the western
Appalachia. The
receptionist at Pine
Meadows Hotel has
a blank stare –
fixated on
something
and nothing
because the
common area
is vacant –
there is a town
resting, and the
work hours begin
regularly but it is
midnight; the
lake by the state
park is smooth
as marble and
there is a glare
of moon light.
The tree frogs have come
out, peeping eerily
to break the
silence for
this quaint town at midnight.

Harrowing

Dry, dead, harrowing
bone. Tainted timbers
of russet and ash. Velvet
carcass caressing the shore.

Fishing lore and an old stock
of news to ignite the fire; It is
already getting late and the line
remains stiff and uninterrupted.

Old man Sally flicks his butane –
silver metal reflects, shining,
piercing flames say good night
to old man Sally;

out like a dead flame,
and his lore, tackled,
holds tight to the Salmon on its
reel and the dry, dead carcass

of the Marlin fish lies still in the
good, cool night as the first spray
of the salty sea puts out the fire.

How to Proceed

Everything is perfect.
Like perfectly winning

And accepting our losses
Perhaps time and time

Again, until each one
Feels a little lighter

A little more bearable
And deeper still:

A search to transcend
Only after having
Known how to proceed.

i in irony

in the irony
of a lowercase, sweet
insignificance.

The hands of a father love
his daughter

Freed doves
yesterday trained –
fly back to their cages

Twenty degree weather
he sports a tee &
cut-offs above his knees.

The unselfish
find their image
In everything

-&-

A reminder
In the mail
forgotten.

In Conversation

*The rain is such
A drought* the
little girl says
and other oxymorons.

The bitter dryness
and seclusion of
being indoors – a
cause by the rain
(a metaphor among
the silence).

The rain is a drought
her father says *like
love is a red rose*
he eyes her mother –

*conversely, rain is
an exquisite sunshine*
she interjected –
how do you say
says the little girl.

*How can you hate
the rain,* her mother
jokes, *when you love
all the flowers* she says.

*I told you love is a red
Rose* laughs
the father….
Conversely says the daughter
rain is love.

Mango Fruit

He held a slice there –
teeth ripened with
mango juice, lips
perched top to bottom,

on colors vexing red,
blue, golden shell of
the bruised mango fruit –
difficulty penetrating

to the core:
deep center of the
laden mango. Sharing
little of its essence, I

on the outside, wanting
to be between them, the mango
fruit, in him where I
cannot be.

Ripe, whole, completely
yearning mango fruit
glowing around the contours
of his mouth, like curves

angled toward his loins –
dark, ripened, pungent tropical fruit
devoured beneath ember sun
by a native of Costa Rica

on the beach of Montezuma.

Popping Tar Bubbles

I.

Soft bottoms of feet tap the asphalt:
walking a short distance on McHenry's Mill Road.
She stops at the white house with the blue shutters, home
two yards away.
A guard rail rusts, fallen paint chips collect in little piles
beneath the concrete steps, and a side door hangs off
its hinges in spite of the weather.

Black folks sit, reclined, upright or leaned over in chairs.
Silent as the day that brought a sturdy cool breeze.
They gaze endlessly to the rising tide of blue, perched
above the tree line lush with honeysuckle.
Wild berries, red in their newness, shake hands with the
willow tree.

He says *don't got nothing better to do than pop tar bubbles
with your feet?* She nods, remembers the children that were
ushered indoors when her little feet stepped over the
property line. Ignorant, she knew not of the woman's
tears for the eighty-something years she lived before the
time of 1981. By then 89. The little girl thought it would be
nice to play with the girls who looked about her age.

That never happened. They went home while Grandma
rocked her sorrows in a lullaby. The cruelness wept in her
eyes, the little girl's tears, she thought felt the same. She
stared at her feet, Sooty like tar from playing in the road.
She seemed to know something about colorlessness
but the inside being the same. She invited them over for
dinner; the lady she wanted to hug sometime blossomed for
a moment. But that never happened.

II.

More white folks lived over the hill. A boy, a few years older, peddled menacingly. Up, over, the neighbor's hill with the white house and blue shutters. Threw stones at a German Shepherd in the yard of another. Rode his go-cart, dirt bike, 4-wheeler, snow mobile – etcetera, etcetera, until the town grew in fury.

He talked about porn night at his house. His father with the pack of Marlboro in his shirt sleeve, rolled over, tucked away but easily accessible. Mother in tight floral spandex pants, bulged on all sides – Went by the name of Rosie. A truc rcd flower.

The boy snorted: spit phlegm the size of tennis balls. Kicked up the front end of his bike. Called it a wheelie, then spun on end & spiraled the molten tar beneath his tires. Called the neighbor's adopted daughter a bastard, then screeched over the hill, and kicked up dusty stones from his driveway.

III.

The Amish don't have electric, Grandma explained one day. She lived between the little girl's house and the white one with the blue shutters. She stared out the window: saw a black buggy drawn by two black horses. A man and a boy held the reins, wore black oval top hats, black vests over striking blue button-down shirts. Blue brighter than heaven had ever seen.

The girl stared: the horses dropped themselves in the

middle of the road. Kept walking as the carriage tires kicked up tar bubbles; a vehicle pulled over to the right, let them pass, then went their way. They lived as mysteriously as any ghost the strange girl had seen.

They lived over the hill. She knew. *They stick to their old ways of living.* That was explained. The Amish abide by strict rules; no television to watch since they live without electric. Somehow that was possible for them. Only the lord knew how though. That day was the only one the girl had seen of the Amish. But she knew they lived a strange life over the hill, somewhere; their house was not visible from the road. But they owned and farmed all that property over there. Five years later she wondered about them.

IV.

The girl learned things in school her parents never bothered telling her. Things like segregation, then she remembered her grandma telling her about the early years when she drank from a different fountain than the neighbors with the blue shutters. They went to different schools too. The little girl sat beside a girl in social studies; the Amish never showed to learn there.

She inquired about them though: she received blank stares from the other kids in school. It seemed no one else knew about the Amish people either.

Sparrows by the Fire

The apple is sweet
She says, picking

the lint from
her sweater.

The scent of
lavender permeates

the room. A
Sparrow taps on

the glass at the
window sill.

Wants to come in
I think, he laughs.

It's too wet
she says, *they'll be*

building nests in
the chimney again.

Best not to light
a fire he says,

until I clean them
out –

Ah, she says,
Sparrows stay

throughout the winter.
Won't be going South

he agrees, flicks
a light to his corn

pipe – *Sparrows*
wait by the fire

on a cold
dismal night.

Sweet Insignificance

A button tied to
the trousers of
a homeless man.
The thread of a
needle poking
from its pin
cushion of the
lovely house
maid. A solitary
feather of a
frozen little
bird or the
sound of glass
when it shatters:
the coffee mug
from that old
job during secret
Santa and no one
would confess to it.
The Christmas wreath
hung in the attic
or the alley cat
from across the
street, the neighbors
let out. The starch
of a police uniform
because he was
humble.

To be Young Again

He plays by the tree
next to the river

and she swings
by on bike

to laugh haphazardly
to the wind

which is unkempt
and yielding wildly

to the laughter.
Like her hair,

dancing to the
sounds, and her

fingers tap
on the handle –

bars as he leans
closer into her

and laughing
softer now

with his chin
resting on her

shoulder: *let's play
in the river* she says

and he lifts her from
the bike, onto his

back, and they piggy-
back toward the river

forever wishing to
be kids again.

Walking Through Grave Yards

A gray covered sky.
It is August; the duck
pond is vacant.
The heat radiates
over the hillside.
"At Rest" Gardens is silent.
Flowers are abundant.
A World War I Veteran was born 1892;
he passed in 1985.
Another, a World War II
Veteran born 1927
died 1981.
A young couple lay together;
one was only 21 (he)
and the other: 19 – it was 2006.
Passerby speculate a car accident;
they are beautiful with their
portraits engraved on their headstones.
My own Grandfather passed in 2010.
I sit by his grave
and think of all
the others, respectfully
walking through the
graves of the dearly
loved who are gone
but not forgotten.

Yellow Banana Roses

I peel the banana taken from the counter, beside the clear glass vase, filled with four yellow-orange roses. The banana becomes yellow banana roses as one less banana inserts one yellow-orange rose. Inserts itself into the one less rose taken from the clear glass vase sitting on the counter beside the four Danon bananas. Oil penetrates oil on canvas. Life, still without motion – a still life painting, oil on the wall, a painting of a still life painting on the wall, oil on canvas, on the wall. A bowl of bananas and four yellow-orange roses stained on oil, the oil on canvas – a still life painted on the counter beside the four ripe yellow-orange roses without one less banana. A still life painting on the wall of four yellow-orange roses.

Chivalry

Her lips are ginger,
like tea and honey.

She wears finer garments
and counts her money.

She is simply not
ordinary. But laughs

at the poets whose
verses sound like

chivalry and prose.
She comprehends them,

the writer's words as not
his own, but a tiny uni-

verse, constellations in
his head. And she writes

him too, in her diary
of chivalry and prose.

Eliciting LSD

I love knowing,
thinking, feeling
being and believing.

I love that you never
once knew me at all
but stopped by for

a brief moment,
and thought your science
to be something

wonderful when you
drove all that I had
to the point of insanity,

(cognition – a live organ: its own living planet full of
possibilities)

that we little humans
cannot control,
cannot touch, but

can cause ruin, death,
pain and destruction
(did I mention pain?)

For anyone other than
themselves (your children?). They stand
defeated while memories
persist in the very sort

of effort they gave

to steal eternity
from someone

they could not own,
but never thought to cherish
life.

Man creates what he
Longs to destroy:
Everything he can touch.

LOSS

The Auctioneer *Sold*

It is dark again.
The lights waver

in the attic but nothing
remains upstairs.

A hum hisses
in the hall among

exposed wires. A few
stacked ice-trays

crack in the freezer,
and a door remains ajar

behind a metal bed-frame,
with its rusted springs

poking through a moth-bitten
mattress. A scabby pillow,

plucked of its feathers,
rests atop a wooden crate

the mice took over when
my last relative passed.

I pry open the lid
to watch them scatter

beneath their scrap-
paper beds, and imagine

they think the same
way as I do

about the emptiness of pure
description, when nothing is left.

The Portrait: Moment of Reflection

Fragmented spaces
remain vacant between
lines, like memories
behind

a curtain. Fallen,
she leans closer
and sketches a half
wrought design,
searching

those vacant eyes
deep & fiery
juxtaposed –

on the page:
his empty vessel
beneath a canopied coal
mine, *Joe*
deeply smothered.

She thumbs ash
side to side, a short wave
locked tight, behind helmet gear &
goggles to protect the eyes.

A portrait bleeds
moments of
reflection –

when she thought he'd
move mountains,

but to
shamble –

Shambhala or Shangri La?

A new horizon, her fingers stencil
meaning, ready to be covered
with paint.

Mosaic Memorabilia

Like wax paper particles,
a gunshot wound leaves
remnant impressions of despair —
an image stained on the wall,
mosaic memorabilia.

From a need for finality,
and a choice to touch his finger
to the trigger metal clangs his teeth.
my beloved's last breath

painted a shattering portrait in July
when light particles burst across
the horizon, like his soul

performing a melodious tango
above a banner that read:

Happy Independence Day

Jill

A Miata, or a twisted vine
of crumpled metal, enveloped –
concave on its side

she curls her lips
on half bitten pieces, and
rakes the back yard

then, awkwardly slanted –
she rests the still frame, colorless
but the crimson of her ribbons,

a cacophony of illumination
beneath stains of indigo
and strands of metaphors weeping.

Jenny

Classmates since the third
grade. Jenny liked to talk
in class. She enjoyed gossip;
she would turn her head,
at the front of the room,
look at me and wink. A
born entertainer she was.
Silly Jenny, always in
trouble for not paying
attention.

I stayed over her house.
An immaculate home,
fancy garage, big screen
TV. Her bedroom was
the size of New Jersey;
She had Mt. St. Helen
on the floor made of shirts
and accessories.

She cherished
Drew Barrymore; grew
to resemble her too. Jenny had
a lazy left eye; accentuated
the brown in them,
complemented her face.
Some freckles. Blond hair,
But "dirty." A baby-doll style.
(Jenny would have said
Baby-dial). A cut that matched
young Drew, with short tresses
tucked away on one side with
a flower burette. Red puffy lips.

Glossy, porcelain teeth.
She said Drew was yummy.
The girls at the lunch table
said Jenny must be a "lez-bo."
Jenny had large D-size boobs.
We, the girls, admired those;
we were "lez-bos" too.
We were 13 then.

Lost touch in high school.
Then after too.
But I remember Jenny.
The news reporter
may not, but he knew
before I knew:

"A woman was murdered
in down-town Baltimore
this evening as gunshots
took the life of the
victim. More at 10 o' clock."

Her friend, a male, died too.
Jenny had been hit in the
upper body, and her swollen
ripe belly. Nine months. A boy,
17, charged with murder
In the first. Took the lives
of three. There's nothing
poetic about it.

Iron Sheathe

He drove the iron,
clad, rustic bone stead-fast
piercing the cling of hard,

wrought, iron sheathe into the
Braille that was his wife, and etched
one-by-one a letter, to each,

an insignia he wore on his sleeve.
A true brute to drive the nail so hard,
that could have cracked, unlike he

would not. And they too gathered
around her, "a mere rendition of her
Beauty" he said, and he drove

through the last nail that drove the dirt
and cratered with each blow. He would
do it, every inch, solid and grounded.

He knew she waded in the water with
their son; his father was only 19 then;
his birth he could not remember

but what his father could only relate to him.
He then felt she must have helped him
survive: his beloved mother. And he stood
unable to remember – where she remains.

Depression

She lies still like glass.
You can see right through
her; veins are the highway
that traces her mal-
nourished body. She
was diagnosed with
depression, but unlike
the sobbing wet ones,
she read Emily Dickenson
and stood there knowing
just how pitiful is plight
when helpless and alone,
or adrift in some mental sea
with desolate lonely whales
without a mate. She felt
her boney knuckles as she wrote
the endless stream of words
in scribble on paper that could not
catch the ink that bled as she fell
from the top stair where writing
made good company as she knelt
down and hovered over every word
before she plunged and caught,
her window lies in shattered tatters –
depression of glass and body:
translucence that splinters.

RELATIONS

The Night Falling in Upon Us

It was the night
we had sex by the fire
when he told me
he'd fill that role
not like a position
but something more
because I was
already pregnant.
He rolled his cigarette
smelling like pine and ash;
we called this place
"the rock" – our place
among the reservoir
where we'd made love –
the place where we could
feel spent, and alone;
the fire burning in this place –
fat and smooth and curvy
like a voluptuous womb
echoing the dissonant sounds –
water swooshing: a birth
in its newness, its fresh scent
cooing upon my breast.
"I'll look less fat in black" I said,
the night falling in upon us
as he leaned over, flicking the
butt to ash; he pried open
my shirt and kissed my naval,
"it's Wellington" he said,
"if it's a boy – after my father."
And he rolled over. Ass to the wind.
And I sat, shirtless in the night – waiting.

It's a Sin

Writing is sinful.
The way we lust
over each other's
bodies. The way
we transcribe on
paper how we
feel when something
as simple as a touch
has us feel like
exploding –
how we thirst
for more knowledge
and embrace in the
intellect of knowing
how the other
will react to the
touch and the
taste of our skin.
We write each word
with gratification
and intensity –
putting feelings on
paper because together
we make love
and don't regret
one moment of it.

In Another

Seeing through your camouflage
past your superficial tongue;
what you say is make-believe,
you put off indifference –
I know better

And sense your every word
as a kind of counterfeit
obsession with being dominant.
Stolen like dreams.
In the night,

I dig deeper
and find your soul
clutching tea leaves.
For knowledge.
To comprehend –

how a woman
could love you,
you are so foolish.
Love was your genius,
your insight:

that brought happiness,
in another.

I Love the Way

I love the way
water caresses
my skin. How
I can look at
you, noting how
intense I feel, especially
when I've gone
unnoticed. I love
the rough edges of
your finger tips
and the neckline
under your v-neck
tea-shirt; the small
stains beneath your
pockets – just how
hard you'll work, bent
over some carburetor
of some diesel engine.
I love thinking about
poetry and how riddles
spindle from my tongue –
how words can make a
clear distinction between
love and lust – how lust
can be superficial and not
deep or intense enough
and how love is an art
that dangerously communicates
with the soul, and if you
expose yourself to the elements
you will die, because you
are a fragile thing – I love

all the opposites; the abstract
complements human anatomy
and I love your strong will,
determination, your fleeting
thoughts because there is just
too much to do and the time
just isn't enough.

Get Well Soon

I must love the despicable:
Those lies you spoon
Between your lips, and
Poke at with a fork.

I love the way your hands
Touch my neck: reach to be
Inside my throat. And,
The way you hold me

There: my back on the floor —
Imprints of lovely, twirling,
Little O's embossed on my skin.
And I love the backs of your knees;

The way they sweat beneath
The crinkles in your jeans.
I love the hollowness in your eyes,
Lips slightly parted, heavy breathing,

And those yellow roses
In full bloom, red carnations
And a get well card beside my
Hospital bed, but not from you —

And I do not blame you. I knew
You could not have learned
About sweet love when I
Found you stooped over

On the cobblestone street (1987)
With your nose nearly broken,

Breathing down your rugged shirt
That read: *You know what your*
Problem is? You're stupid.

Europa

The extremes of fire and ice
harmonize balance
like queen and king.

The Phoenician beauty,
or the brightest swoon of the solar
system: the stealthy white bull carried

her to the island of Crete. The moonlight
reflected from her young breasts, and Zeus
blazed in a fire of truth; the white bull,

he unveiled and tossed into the cosmos.
Taurus now rules with an Army's tactful eye
and protects his luscious bride –

Queen of Crete, Europa. The icy
crescent moon cradles Jupiter in her
cosmic spiraling center

with her lover Zeus. The Queen
on the island below, and Jupiter's moon
above, create a unison of perfect symmetry.

Embrace

Love is a twisted
Vine: ivy and sumac
clung to the tree trunk
where without such
splendor – those most
dangerous things could
not survive; the strength
of another provides
the life line
of the small
and precious, lively
little leaves –
brute strength and witty
character create the
passion that is the
fruit of existing
together, to conquer
what would not be
without the loving
wit of ivy, cloaked in
the embrace of an
oak tree.

Wishing Window

I tilt my face
toward the sun.

My window is down;
he will not let go.

Not tonight. It is
evening – the sun

is at dusk, on the
wane to shed

light on the moon.
The breeze is getting

heavier, despite his
slowing down.

I shuffle my feet;
his grip gets

tighter but he's
afraid; the

moon moves in
closer like peering

through my window
at his balled-up fist

clutching my jeans
but I cannot

help, this time
will be my last –

wishing through
this window

that he would
just let go.

To Dance

Love, or spinnerets
striking a chord with
an accordion – woven
between sound and
satisfied starvation –
giving in, and up,
everything on the fly –
keeping what is wholesome
in its thread and to
play louder – a harmony
or a tune that, corrected,
once gone wrong can
forgive totally and utterly
or find some other sound
which to meet at one
another's alter; the music
that plays so familiar
and time to dance, clutched,
in an embrace so belonging
into their arms and
the only fear is not
knowing how a single
little day would be spent –
never having been
at this altar.
Love is bringing them here.
Love is how.
Love is here. Love is harmony. Peace.

Untitled

It is the mind again.
The past bringing
itself to the forefront:
thoughts hindering on
obligation. It is
October; the fish
are stirring up mud.
The receding shore
evokes a memory
of all things to come
again but not suddenly –
only a matter of time,
then change. Floundering
thoughts are the highway
of utopia. The serotonin
cannot rest. Sugar cannot
resist. Something to bring
on the reverie of when
there was blue-grass
and guitar: a couplet
to talk over the fire.
Love dies, I know.
But nothing holds
against me so tightly
but the constant hum
of your strings –
the hollow of your shell.

Acceptance

Invasive, like
Cancer – tumors
That fill my bladder,
My breasts, my spine –
My whole self-cloaked

With regret, but I had
Little to keep me there
In that place among
The webs of our
Dissatisfaction-

Our whole place together,
Dysentery, sterile,
(But my spine)
Exposed to the disease

Knowing this too is not
Meant to last.

Karaoke

And you laced me down, salted

My naval, while I fed you lemons

With fingers tipping the tequila -

Yesterday

When you hear my anger
realize you've done
something to intrigue me.

And when you touch my
tears, pull away, because
you meant something else.

If you embrace the wreckage,
the tension will dissolve in
a smooth texture of melted butter.

And when the warmth fades,
you'll hear laughter, and
remember our ability
to deal with the pain.

When you return to see
the faucet still dripping
in the kitchen you left spotless
the evening you walked

out our door: think disorder
began when you turned those pages
that had spaces to be filled.

And when you touch the moment
and remember you wanted today
more than anything else

you'll hear the silence
and believe there was no need
to be anywhere else.

METAPHYSICS

In a Grain of Rice

The stale taste of sugar.
Metal, Mercury, and most
Of all: Love. To sense, is to
Feel; is to live
Fully in the clutch of existence.

Purity; is a solitary
Grain of rice without
Its fill of the others;
On an empty plate
With space to grow

Fuller, lively, not
Expecting much
But to be alone
Here and now
Curled in upon itself:

A mere speck, like
Dust, with seemingly
No purpose
But the quintessential
Place for being.

Finding God

I was afraid
until I finally
found God; he
took me lovingly
into his arms
and told me stories
about others who
are like myself.
I told God
that I do not
like the grays
and mirrors –
that they remind
me too much
of myself and
I feel totally
Inadequate at
times to belong to
anything meaningful,
then God raised
his fist – told me
meaning is in
anything
alive and the
inanimate is just
a token for caring
a little too much.

Inner Sanctum

You have to find
an inner sanctuary.

Where the mind
can settle, and beauty

can exist; like
walking through

wildflowers of
an inner sanctum

where there is the
freedom to grow

and to persist –
like taking an

extra long breath
and venting for a few

extra seconds during
the letting go phase

of life and reality.
Where the most

Ideal things can
take precedence.

The Devil's Resurrection

Dead stars fall,
land like ash
in the tomb of
a rotting tray.

The leaves are gray.
Nothing beautiful
sheds their light
to let the beauty remain.

That poor, empty,
lost little man had been
a somebody once.
The heavy blankness

where his eyes had been
leaves his gray suit to
dry in the mud. The rain
rinsed where the stain

had been, that once was a
soul-full man now turned
to ashes, mere dust of a
hollow man. Empty shell,

the soul carved out his
eyes; the hollowness
lingers: Exoskeleton
rough on the edges.

Look through the
tunnel of dark,

empty, space – the void
of eternity, nothingness,
suction, a vacuum into

an eternal endless drift,
a pit to nowhere. It's cold
in there. The carcass,
just carrion, plucked

from his gray suit.
An end where there
had been no beginning,
A resurrection wasted.

I stared into the heavy
blankness of his hollowed-
out eyes as I plucked
dead crickets from

the window sill-
their empty cavity,
exoskeleton, dry
and bound to
disintegrate.

Nothing good comes
from there. He was
lost. Drained of his
instincts for breathing
life.

And I found his soul:

a reflection from
the window pane when
I plucked each one
Into the dirt:

tink, tink, tink

to watch them
give life again-
even in the
minuteness
of detail.

Timelessness

There is no beginning
nor an end. There is
perpetual motion like
the cycling of the seasons.
The waves of life reach
depths like the sea
where biology cannot
touch life's continuations
because what is
metaphysical can only
be touched by abstractions;
one may view life through
an objective lens but not
all things are concrete –
like vibrations, sound
waves, lightning and
speed. We venture this
life as humans until we
touch the dirt and from
our bodies grows the
wildflowers from which
the insects feed – and only
then we become all things
(physical) as our Spirit departs –
an energy vibration like
the sound and speed of light:
quietly unnoticed, uninterrupted.

White Noise from a Cemetery in Lonaconing

He had been in a state
of purgatory where

he could not rest,
but languished

between restlessness
from a resentful conscience

and the soil eroding
beneath his feet.

He envisioned himself
as a boy again,

with his grandfather
who'd kick-up

the earth, during his
little league game.

And he recalls when
Grandfather said

that his life
was unlike the years

when the earth clung to his cleats –
before his own grandfather

died, and he turned

over his ratty glove

to mow at the cemetery
and pay off his father's debt.

And during their
last dinner together,

his own father crossed
his arms and rolled his eyes back

and spoke of timelessness
beyond the white noise

of his father's
grave, where

whipping willows whistle
in a field, a meadow,

a pond, a lake and
cicadas create

a cadence beyond
the meadow trees

where spring peepers peep
and he would play little league

with the soil eroding
beneath his feet.

And with his arms folded
and his eyes rolled back,

he examined the lightness
of being consciously

exchanging seventy years
for his cleats.

RUIN

Condemned

Someone lived here once.
In this place among
the broken lightbulbs
tattered on the front
porch, its lantern still

strung by the thread
that is hung among
the shards of glass –
ready to break free
from its hinges.

A door, remaining ajar,
holds steady in the fog
where the cobwebs
string together its
artifacts: half cracked

pots, frames without
a mirror, rags of dolls
and the spider-laden
mattresses. I imagine,
taking this photograph,

the hefty wood is solid
as its life had been
when there was a
seamstress – when
knitted scarves hung

in the attic that were
taken out on Christmas

and the ghosts adorned
the halls in October
before the entire five

bedroom gave way
to old age, famine,
disease or plain ol'
departure: before ruin –
when the seemingly

dated dwelling had been
a refuge: a home
when artwork adorned
the walls too and
the halls smelled

better – something of cooking
like butter. Cinnamon
decorated crescent rolls,
and the moon only gave
way to the night

in the shadows by the fire.
And there, by the light
of night they sang

songs that only this
home can remember,

perhaps, in its memory,
are better times.

Posted

Do not pass here
in this place
among the ruin.

Its eighteenth
century wooden
exterior gave way

into the burden
of evolution –
a revolution of time

as the door way
began to sag
because no longer

do children pass through
its doors to huddle
by the fire.

Which used to smoke;
the fire logs
taken down

by hand-held axes
by those
whose fingers

swelled into blisters
before machines
could build.

This home is still —
nestled in a land-
scape of pine

and forest when
an outhouse stood
cold in its winter

frozen tundra like
a lake that could
not be broken because

its roots bore too deep.
This home, erected
when there was a garden

tended by a misses
before factory farming –
the land provided them.

This home is in ruin
in a memory before
electricity, shambles

collect at your feet
when you stand in
awe at the entry-way

where its posted
not to enter
because to enter

is at your own risk
because here lies
the past

in a grave
of wood-plastered
mortar –

not withstanding
the strength
of nature

ravishing its bare
naked bones.

When will its ruin
go unnoticed?

Rusty Valves of a Spent Machine

Once was making progress
sits in rust and ruin
among the rubble of concrete
that appears like ash.

The quarry outside its broken
metal frame, hosts
the dive school
who take in their surroundings;

Graffiti tags the cement
block foundation: peace signs
dredging up the past and lovers'
whose initials mark the time.

All who had been there took
a piece of the rubble, tossing
pebbles into the water
like a wishing well, pondering

the old; a rustic electrical panel
overgrown by the trees
once gave life to the
now dead machine –

a lingering sentiment
of rust-covered ruin.
A life without motion
is a spent machine.

HOME

Dwellings

The home is a fortress
to protect against
the elements.

The best place to hide
is often the bedroom
beneath the mounds
of sheets collected
by the bed.

Not like the fox does
which hides in the
fortress of a den
to keep away those
predators – the snake.

A dwelling is a burrow
to raise our young
and to watch them
play beneath their
camp-style tents.

A dwelling bears witness
to the conditions they
serve to protect – the fox
huddles there in camp-
style leaves packed by mud.

To each there is a style –
those dwellings that
give shadow to twilight
staying cool then warm

again: our make-shift

canopy in a starry night.
A dwelling is a home
where the trees provide
all that is plentiful –
none shall go wasted.

He Called it Daniel's Den

The cats occupy the bed.
Outside is night; there's
an abundance of them

here, lining the shore
in the tatters of sea
and weed: a mermaid's

purse, stones jeweled
in the glint of the light
tower, and shambles

of once perfectly unbroken
shells: clams and oysters
amiss in the debris.

A stingray, upside down,
with a mouth full of jelly –
and the ocean foaming

in nettles of grainy salt.
The home he called Daniel's
Den, illuminated by moon,

is blue, beautiful blue,
like the Atlantic
out its doors

and decorated of fishing
lore: nets hung, strung
on the wall,

a puffer fish from taxidermy
its razor, edge, teeth cuts
fiercely into the flesh

if one was to touch them.
The Marlin fish and fake
talking, singing, bass and

the dangling of ornaments of
Star fish hanging like a
Night sky over the

cast iron furnace – used
for nothing but decoration
like a chimney for lovers.

We were to get married here
before he died;
Grandad's home was the

refuge of forgiveness – the
sea to wash away pains
of the New Year, giving

way to summer – tossing
the glass bottle with a note
into a jade-colored marine

hoping all would feel right
again, but he died there in a pool
of constellations; he'd point one

out and tell you to make a
wish – and it was for that
week to never end; I was

only eleven; the evening
when we devoured the
Milky Way and sent the

night, Orion's Belt, our prayers
and we'd walk the beach,
our feet to-the-sand,

of hope, collecting broken
purses, never to find a shark
tooth, thinking life is fair

because life was around us –
it was everywhere,
but I didn't think to

wish he'd never die
because he was Grandad –
invincible, not like

the divine, but like
Tarzan, hanging from its
branches, in the tree of life.

Giving me the power to
hope and dream knowing
that moment would inspire

more than a monetary value
of dead fish, but memories
in life and death –

of being alive, like the
tiny, baby stirring in my
abdomen and the kitten

cooing back in bed –
he would have called
him Midnight,

and laugh his hearty
laugh because he
would be purring

so loud, and
Midnight would walk
into the night

to the Carolina shore
in the clear, cool
night

and wish to be near him
again, this time.

Invested in a City

In the majesty of light
there is something celestial –
making progress, building
and erecting towers of glass.

The city is alone at night
where the eyes cannot see
its suburbs on the corner.
The tax payers sip from

Cappuccinos beneath the paper
bound at their fingers. Wall Street
doesn't die you know if crashing
means to still be alive tomorrow.

Each row of homes stands amid
the newness of condominiums
where raising babies is to walk
out the front door amid construction.

"We love it here", she says and the
playground is centered
and proud – a city of sprawling detail.
They will never be alone here.

Because the city is a place
amid hopes and dreams
going off like light
are the ideas of men

and women alike, in each
they embrace, sinking their

hearts into something fabulous
like Grand Central Station.

Engineered and erected within
the city are walls of glass
and they can forget themselves
awhile.

MEDITATIVE

Dawn

A rose-colored garland
and moss covered streets.

Litter in the blackened alley.
A turquoise-pierced sky.

Glints of rain against
shards of glass.

And an opaque frost;
It's turning to January.

The lights are off
The street light flickers

Fire light does the same.
It's warm inside

And as far as she can see
Looking beyond the window

It's early, not yet twilight
But the shimmers of light

Cast in her the confidence
That the setting of dawn

Brings out the sun
And all will be

Alive again.

Beauty in the Deadliest of Things

There is a Northern breeze
through the open window;
the white satin curtains
sway subtly affront the
cottage's interior, adorned
with silver, metal frames
where the young miss writes
poetry in her journal; the leather
binding is etched with an owl
and the sea birds flap
their wings in the gusty
breeze. Soft branches of
trees swing rhythmically
in the tropics.
She writes about fireflies
that scuttle their wings
hovering above the pond –
mosquitoes made nests
and Geese flocked over head
above signs that read:
do not feed. At the swamp
preservation the wetlands
are home to carnivorous
plants – the greenness of the
grasshopper upon the pitcher
plant looks plentiful to its
awaiting bulb.
The miss went to visit there
once in the Western region of
Maryland where she hoped
to find her solitude for writing.
The vacation, being over, she

returned home to speak eloquently
of nonfiction – a daily entry
for a magazine where she submits
and looks back to the days
of the Appalachia where she
met her husband-to-be and
he found, in her, her beauty
like gardens of the mossy green
as the front door opens
and the scent of lavender
permeates the room
like the honeysuckle in their
memories; supple and sweet
are those images he holds
of the plant devouring
the insect that wriggled
in nectar-sweet honey
and he smiles as he looks
at her, pondering the beauty
of those deadly things.

In a Willow Tree

I found, in the glint
of Twilight, a pendant

enamored in Gold
like topaz

hanging from the branch
of a Willow Tree.

The Topaz stone shone
like an Iris from the garden,

beset with diamonds, but
slightly tarnished

from the weather.
I imagine it belonged

to her once, and wonder
in awe if she placed

it upon her neck —
a gift from him;

why a topaz yellow stone
and from whom?

Did she find her way
to the dance hall

in a matching gown
and is she still there,

I ask myself, marveling
in its exquisite detail

and how has it come to be
here among this willow branch

where the Starling flutters
from its branches

to caw overhead
and I leave it there

to be pondered by another,
a passerby who can see

it in awe too like the Starling
had, when she landed there

and I happened to notice too.
The pendant belonged to

someone once: who is she?
And where did she go?

Refuge

A Condemned house
on the hill.
A refuge for
Birds; from the
Beautiful bay window
a pigeon looks out
at the pedestrians
and passerby who's
not looking from their
glass exteriors.
While willow branches
perch alongside grassy
garlands, and nests are
being built from the rafters,
where sparrows fit slits
of hay in cracks among
the floor boards, and the
pigeons nestle among
squirrel huts: mounds of
dry leaves in the walls.
While the mail man keeps
going by, it's unoccupied
place gone unnoticed,
but the alley cat scurries –
darts among the weeds,
heading toward the open door,
otherwise, keeping its place
in the guest house.
The birds haven't yet noticed.

Wild

Somewhere
there's a storm.
But not here.

Not in this place
that blooms with sensation –
my senses are startled
by the Raven, ahead.

No one mows here.
There's no pruning of
hedges of tree-lined streets.

All is wild.
Wild like the dandelions.
Wild as fire
Wild like the call
of the crow: the caw
of a cat.

In the wild
there is an expanse
of pastel. Of blue
a hue like green –
a painted landscape,
not hung on the wall:

no trophy of foliage,
fawn, or fern.
Just the wild.
Uninhibited. But
somewhere in the wild
there's a storm.

Because the Raven
is steady,
looking.

Then, there's a call
from within,
the wild.

And the Raven takes cover.
Because all is wild.

Epilogue

Candace Meredith

About the Author

Candace Meredith earned her Bachelor of Science degree in English Creative Writing from Frostburg State University in the spring of 2008. Her works of poetry, photography and fiction have appeared in literary journals Bittersweet, Backbone Mountain Review, Anthology 17, Greensilk Journal and The Broadkill Review. She currently works as a Freelance Editor for an online publishing company and has earned her Master of Science degree in Integrated Marketing and Communications (IMC) from West Virginia University. Her first effort in writing a collaborative children's book is a progress in the making and Candace anticipates seeing completion of the book in 2017.

Visit Candace's Author Page At:

www.ctupublishinggroup.com/candace-meredith.html

Acknowledgements

• To be Young Again and Sweet Insignificance published 2016 by The Broadkill Review

• Saying it Simply, Invertebrates, and The Auctioneer *Sold* published in Backbone Mountain Review 2009, 2013, 2016

• Jill published in Bittersweet of Frostburg State University in 2008

• Yesterday published in the Greensilk Journal 2017

• i in irony, Arts Poetica, and The Portrait: Moment of Reflection published in Anthology 17 2017

About the Book

Every once in a while you stumble upon something incredibly special and unique. If you are reading this poetry collection you are one of the lucky ones.

These thoughts are profound - exploring worlds of nothingness and the empty spaces people used to occupy. Ghost memories, barely there yet impossible to ignore. Verse that is personal, emotive, intimate, explosive and intense. Poetry about the rough and tumble of lust, the symmetry of love, the wreckage when it all goes bad.

At times abstract, spinning through inner and outer energies towards places that, once upon a time, were people; now ruins, left to turn to dust seemingly in the blink of an eye. Foundations sustained by better days but ravaged by age and tempestuous weather, a sparkling gold universe turned to decay.

Candace Meredith has perfected her craft and turned something otherwise ordinary into something extraordinary. Her words paint pictures and bring forth memories, long hidden. She writes moments that take your breath away, her sentences are velvet.

- L. J. Diaz, author of *Catching Snowflakes*

www.ctupublishinggroup.com

Creative Talents Unleashed is an independent publishing group that offers writers an opportunity to share their writing talents with the world. We are committed to fostering and honoring the work of writers of all cultures.

For More Information Contact:

info@ctupublishinggroup.com

76404756R00066

Made in the USA
Columbia, SC
04 September 2017